French

Learn French In 21 DAYS!

A Practical Guide To Make French Look Easy! EVEN For Beginners

Table Of Contents

Introduction

This book contains 21 lessons to help you learn French quickly.

At the start of this book you will find tips on how to learn French fast. You will also get to understand the French culture, and differences between English and French. Furthermore, you can get started with the French alphabet and practice your pronunciation.

In the next part of the book, you will be able to memorize the numbers in French and learn how to say the date and time. You will also learn and memorize the most common French words and phrases.

The next several chapters go even deeper into the French language, namely gender and articles, nouns and pronouns, adjectives and adverbs, and how to form demonstratives, possessives, interrogatives, and negations.

Finally, you will immerse yourself in the prepositions, verbs, tenses, and imperatives of the French language. You will also encounter common travel and business phrases that you can use in everyday life.

This book is concise and incredibly useful for those who want to learn French quickly and efficiently. You can study each chapter together with an efficient learner's dictionary and just about any other online French language learning application.

Let's begin the journey.

Chapter 1: How to Learn French FAST

To learn French fast, you must put your heart and soul into it. In other words, you need to have the desire to not just speak and understand, but also to live and breathe in French. It is not difficult to do this, after all, since it is a beautiful language.

The first step to learning any language is to find out your learning style. Some people learn faster than others because they have already identified whether they learn faster by reading or by listening to audio tapes. You can take an online test on learning styles to determine yours.

The next step is to figure out how you were able to acquire the language or languages that you already know. Some people started out by listening to tons of songs and by reading a lot of interesting books in the language. You can also repeat the same techniques for this goal.

Next, you need to have the discipline to immerse yourself completely in the language in the next 21 days. It takes at least 21 days of repetitively doing something in order to turn it into a habit, and if you want to learn fast you need to practice every single day; if possible, all the waking hours of each day.

Start by learning at least 30 French words every day. You can get them from this book, and then build upon your collection using any English to French dictionary out there, starting with the most common words and phrases. Give yourself a test every day or have someone test you to help you recall and retain the words that you have learned.

Grammar is essential to learning any language, and French is no exception. That is why this book is focused on helping you learn the structure of the French language. Understand how the different components in a sentence are put together.

Aside from studying with this book, you should also go the extra mile by getting yourself immersed in the language. This can be done by watching French movies with French captions (not English!) and reading French books, starting with the children's books. You should also listen to French songs and audiobooks, and keep a French journal in which you can practice expressing your thoughts in French. If you have access to an online French grammar checker, or if you have a French speaking friend, have them check your journal and pronunciation.

As soon as you have a good grasp of French grammar and a more substantial vocabulary, start speaking in French as often as you can. Find a French chatmate online and practice with him or her whenever you can. Be prepared to be corrected many times and take everything in as a learning experience. If you do not have anyone to speak with in French yet, simply talk to yourself out loud and record your voice so that you can check if you are indeed doing a good job.

Exercise

Enumerate all of the tips that you should follow in order to learn French fast. Write them down on a sheet of paper and then compare your list with what was written in this chapter. Post the list somewhere that is easily visible to you every day.

Chapter 2: The French Culture

When you think about French culture, what is the first thing that comes into your mind? Some people would associate it with images of the Eiffel tower and the Louvre, while others would think of fashion, food, and art. Naturally, there is a lot more to the French culture than what you might get out of movies and the television.

It would be impossible to summarize the entirety of the French culture in a single chapter, so take the following tidbits as a simple overview.

One thing to remember about the French culture is that the French are very proud of their government and nation, and any negative comments toward these would be seen as offensive.

French cuisine is esteemed worldwide and has influenced many other cuisines from around the world. Some of the most famous dishes that the French have contributed to the world and have become classics are the coq au vin, boeuf bourguinon, and of course, the creme brulee.

The French are also passionate and romantic by nature, and by this they are open towards the concept of extramarital affairs. In fact, approximately 50 percent of the children in France are born to parents who are unmarried.

Art and France have been married for centuries, especially in the major cities. The public buildings and cathedrals in France clearly display this. The Venus de Milo and the Mona Lisa, two of the most famous works of art, are displayed in the Louvre Museum.

Paris is the most prominent beacon of high-end fashion and has shared to the world the works of Louis Vuitton, Dior, Chanel, and Hermes. You can even see it in such fashion words as "chic", "haute couture", and "avante garde".

As for the holidays in France, keep in mind that most of the French are Catholics and therefore celebrate Christmas, Easter, and other traditional Christian holidays. The 1st of May is the Labor Day of the French, while on May 8 they celebrate the Victory in Europe Day. July 14 is when they celebrate Bastille Day.

Whatever your passion may be, you will find it in the culture of the French. By allowing yourself to sink deeper into their culture you will find that learning the language is simply a bonus in the entire experience.

Exercise

Create a list of the aspects of the French culture that you like the most. It may be their cuisine, fashion, food, art, or even their passion and romance. After that, make an" inspiration board" by compiling pictures and French phrases that are associated with the items on your list. Use this to help keep you determined to learn the French language.

Chapter 3: The Differences between English and French

Before jumping into your French lessons, it is important to understand the differences between the English language and the French language. Take note that English and French have a lot of similarities in terms of grammar and vocabulary, so it is not as hard to learn it as you might think.

For instance, French and English both have 26 letters, but French also has letters that have diacritics, which are: é è à ù ç â ê î ô û ë ï ü. There are many differences in the sounds between French and English, and it is here where beginners usually commit both spelling and pronunciation errors.

Articles in the French language are more common than in English. The same is true for Roman numerals, while the reverse is true when it comes to capitalization.

Conjugations in French are one of the most challenging to the French learner, because each conjugation is different for every grammatical person, while in English it is only different for the third person singular. Take note as well that the gender of the words plays a critical role in expressing oneself in the English language.

When it comes to negation, the French use two words, while in English only one is used. Silent letters are very common in French, and the most interesting thing is that they are not the same letters.

As you continue to study French, you will encounter more differences between the languages that you previously had not noticed. This is perfectly alright for as long as you are aware of these differences and aim to not confuse yourself between the two languages. Constant practice is what helps you to become more fluent and accurate in this beautiful language.

Exercise

Recall as many of the differences between French and English as stated in the chapter. Compare your answers with the chapter's content. Reflect on how you can overcome these obstacles.

Chapter 4: French Alphabet and Pronunciation

Remember when you were a kid and you had to learn your ABCs? Pretend that you are back in the kindergarten classroom with your crayons and tracing paper, but this time you have an attractive French teacher in front of the class. You want to be curious and eager to please your teacher, so pay full attention to *L' Alphabet*.

The French Alphabet

One thing that the French language has in common with English is that it has 26 letters in its alphabet. However, many of them are pronounced quite differently.

But before you delve deep into the French alphabet, take note that there are "accentuated vowels" and special characters that are not found in written English. These are:

- The grave accent è, which sounds like the "e" in the word "bet". It is also found in the vowels "a"and "u".

- The accute accent é, which sounds like "ei". It can only be found above the letter e.

- The circumflex accent ê, which is placed over all vowels. It causes the vowel to sound longer, such as the "ay" in "play".

- The French /ə/, which is a unique sound that sounds like a short "u" sound.

- The cedilla, which turns the "k" sound into the "s" sound. For example, the French word "garçon" (which means boy or waiter) is pronounced as /GHAR son/.

- The diaeresis (called "tréma" in French), which is placed on the second of two consecutive vowels. It is to show that the vowels are pronounced separately. For example, the French word for Christmas, Noël, is pronounced as /nou EL/.

To help you understand these unique French sounds better, go online and listen to them using free applications such as Google Translate.

Now, practice saying the following letters based on the description below each. Keep in mind that the words used to help describe the sounds are based on the Standard American English accent.

Aa /ah/

Sounds like the "a" in "father".

Bb /bé/

Sounds like the "e" in "bed".

Cc /sé/

Sounds like "k", but if there is a cedilla, it becomes the sound "s".

Dd /dé/

Sounds like

Ee /ə/

Sounds like the "a" in "again".

Ff /ef/

Sounds like the "f" in "food".

Gg / g/

Sounds like the "s" in "measure" if it comes after "e" or "i". Other than that, it sounds like the "g" in "girl".

Hh /ashe/

It is often not pronounced. For example, "heureux", which is French for "happy", is pronounced as /EUH reuh/.

Ii /ee/

Sounds like the "ee" in "seen".

Jj /dji/

Sounds like the second "g" in "garage".

Kk /ka/

Sounds like the "k" in "kite".

Ll /el/

Sounds like the "l" in "love".

Mm /em/

Sounds like the "m" in "man".

Nn /en/

Sounds like the "n" in "neck".

Oo /o/

Sounds like the "o" in "holiday".

Pp /pe/

Sounds like the "pe" in "pellet".

Qq /ku/

Sounds like the "k" in "kick".

Rr /er/

Sounds like the "r" in "error".

Ss /ess/

Sounds like the "s" in "sat".

Tt /te/

Sounds like the "t" in "tent".

Uu /y/

A uniquely French sound, which is similar to the "oo" in "too".

Vv /ve/

Sounds like the "v" in "vow".

Ww /doblé vee/

Sounds like the "w" in "weekend".

Xx /iks/

Sounds like the "x" in "xylophone".

Yy /y/

Pronounced as /I grec/ when alone. Other than that, it is like the sound "ea" in "each".

Zz /zed/

Sounds like the "z" in "zebra".

French Pronunciation Guidelines

➢ If two /k/ sounds are together, only the first one is not changed, such as accepter /AK sep tee/ ("accept").

➢ The sound /ks/ becomes /z/ or /gz/, such as exact /EG zakt/.

➢ If the sounds /k/ and /g/ precede "e" or "i", they become /s/ and /ʒ/, respectively.

➢ If the letters "gu" is succeeded by "e" or "i", the /u/ is silent., such as guerre /GEH/ ("war").

➢ If the "s" is between vowels, it becomes /z/, such as chose /shooz/ ("thing").

➢ The /t/ becomes /s/ if followed by "ie", "ia", and "io", such as patient /PEH syun/ ("patient").

➢ If the word-final /il/ comes after a vowel, it becomes /ee/, such as œil /uh Y/ ("eye").

➢ If "ill" is not at the start of a word, it turns into /ee/, such as oreille /ooh REYH/ ("ear").

➢ If no vowel is placed before "ill", the sound /i/ is pronounced, such as fille /fee yh/ ("girl"). However, the /l/ is pronounced in the words distiller /distile/ ("to distill") and mille /mil/ ("thousand").

➢ If the letter "o" comes after the letter "y", it is pronounced as /wa/, such as voyage /VWA yaj/ ("travel").

➢ If "i", "u", and "y" are placed before a vowel in a word, they become glides, such as pied /pye/ ("foot"), oui /wi/ ("yes"), and huit /oo weet/ ("eight").

➢ The final "e" is not pronounced, such as bouche /boosh/ ("mouth").

18

➤ In French there is a phenomenon called "liaison", wherein a consonant which is usually silent is pronounced right before the word that it precedes. For example, "vous avez" is pronounced as /vou zavee/ ("you have").

➤ Also, when a word ends with a silent "e", the liaison is present in the vowel that follows it. For example, reste à cote is pronounced as /rest eeah cotee/ ("stay next").

➤ "Enchaînement" is another French language phenomenon and it involves transferring the consonant sound at the end of a word to the start of the word that it precedes. For instance, elle est is pronounced as /e le/ ("she is").

➤ Most of the time, the final e in French words is not pronounced. For example: jambe /jamb/ (leg), bouche /bush/ (mouth), lampe /lamp/ (lamp).

➤ If the e is followed by a double consonant, it becomes the sound /ei/, but more open and without the glide from e to i. For example: pelle /pèl/ (shovel), lettre /lètr/ (letter)

➤ Memorize the mute consonants in the French language, which are: the final -b that follows an m- (such as plomb /ploh/ [metal]), final -d (such as chaud /shoh/ [warm]), final -p (such as trop /tro/ [very much]), final -s (such as trés /treh/ [very much]), final -t (such as part /par/ [part]), final -x (such as prix /pri/ [price]), and the final -z (such as assez /ase/ [enough]).

Pronunciation of the Single Vowels

/a/ -sounds like the first /a/ in marmalade, but not as open. The more open vowel sound that is similar to this one is â.

Examples: table (table), chat (cat), sac (bag), baggage (luggage), rat (rat), matin (morning), bras (arm)

/e/ -sounds like the the English indefinite article 'a' but make the sound sharper, such as the second /a/ in marmalade. Sounds that are similar to this one are /eu/ which is a more open e and /oeu/ which is a more open eu.

Examples: deux (two), oeuvre (master works), cheveu (hair), soeur (sister), beurre (butter), heure (hour)

Keep in mind that the final e in French words is always silent. For example: Notre Dame, Anne

Also, the e in the middle of a French word is glided over. For example: boulevard, Mademoiselle

/i/ -sounds like the /ee/ sound in the English language but shorter.

Examples: courir (to run), pipe (pipe), midi (midday), minute (minute), nid (nest)

/o/ -there are two different sounds with the letter o in French. The first sound is an open /o/ that sounds like the o in the following English words: not, more, and for.

The second sound is a more closed /o/ like the one in the English low and go.

Majority of the /o/ sounds in French pronunciation are open. It is only closed when it is placed at the end of the word.

Examples of the open /o/: boote (boote), homme (man), développer (to develop)

Examples of the closed /o/: indigo (indigo), vélo (bicycle)

Sounds that are similar to the closed /o/ are /eau/, /au/, and /ô/. For example: auto (car), contrôle (control), and eau (water)

/u/ -the French pronunciation for u is not actually present in the English language. While the English pronunciation of /u/ is the sound of it in the word push, in French it is quite different. However, the u in push is present in the French language, but it is for the vowel combination /ou/.

Examples: minute, voiture (car), humain (human)

/y/ -the pronunciation of this is similar to the French double /i/ sound.

Examples: loyer /loi ier/ (lease), noyer /noi ier/ (to drown), rayer /rai ier/ (to scratch), pays /pai i/ (country)

Practice pronouncing the following:

si	sou	su
rue	rit	roue
sous	assure	assis
écrou	écrit	écru
repu	tous	asile

tisse	sucre	rousse
git	joue	jus
revit	revue	couve

Accentuated Vowels

One of the most obvious differences between English and French is that the latter uses accented characters. Most vowel sounds, with the exception of /y/, can be accentuated.

/è/ -this is pronounced like the /e/ in pet. The grave accent is also placed on top of a as well as u to create à and ù, respectively, although these do not change the pronunciation.

Examples: Hélène /hei len/ (Helen), où /oo/ (where)

/é/ -the special character above the e is called the acute accent and it is only used over e.

Example: égoïst /ei guist/ (selfish), comédie /ko mei dee/ (comedy)

/ê/ -the circumflex accent, which is the special character over e, can also be placed on top of all the other vowels. What it does is that it lengthens the sound.

Example: à côté de /ah co ti du/ (beside), plaît /ple/ (please)

/ë/ -this special character is called the dieresis mark and it is placed over a vowel to show that the sound is a separate syllable from the other vowel next to it. For instance, if you have two vowel put together such as ai, it is usually pronounced as /e/, but if you place a dieresis on top of the /i/, the sound becomes /ai/.

Example: naïf /na eef/ (naive), haïr /a eer/ (to hate).

Vowel Combination Pronunciation

/ou/ -this vowel combination sounds like something in between the sounds of the u in bush and the oo in cool.

Example: cou /coo/ (neck), genou /zhu noo/ (knee)

/au/ and /eu/ -this is pronounced the same way as /ô/.

Example: bateau /bah too/ (ship), eau /oo/ (water)

/oi/ -to pronounce this vowel combination, make the /wa/ sound.

Example: doigt /doo wa/ (finger), oie /oo wa/ (goose)

/ai/ -this is pronounced the same way as /ê/.

Example: j'ai /zhei/ (I have), maison /mei sohn/ (house)

/ui/ -to produce the sound of this vowel combination, the diphthong /oo wee/.

Example: fruit /froo ee/ (fruit), aujourd'hui /oo zhoor dui/ (today)

/eu/ and /oeu/ -pronounced the same way as the short /u/ sound.

Example: bleu /blu/ (blue), feu /fu/ (fire)

/er/, /et/ and /ez/ -these vowl combinations have a sound that is similar to /é/.

Example: boulanger /boo lan zhee/ (baker), hier /ee ye/ (yesterday

Practice pronouncing the following:

mêle	meule	molle
coeur	corps	caire
sol	sel	seule
Plaire	pleure	implore
l'or	l'air	leur
peur	port	père
gueule	guerre	encore

Nasal Vowel Pronunciation

/on/ - it is not possible to find an exact English sound that is similar to this unique French sound. However, the closes vowel would probably be the long /o/ such as the o in long (but without fully pronouncing the /ng/ sound).

Example: oncle /ohng klu/ (uncle), bon /bohn/ (good)

/an/ and /am/ -if a vowel combination is followed by the letter n or m, it does not immediately mean that the sound would be nasal, unless the n or m is the final letter of the word. However, if there is only one vowel before the n or m, the vowel is a nasal sound.

Example: détient /dee chanh/ (holds), sens /sahns/ (sense)

/en/ and /em/ -the closest sound that is similar to these French nasal vowels would be the a in swan.

Example: souvent /soo vahn/ (often), ensemble /ahn sahm blu/ (together)

/in/, /ain/, /ein/, and /aim/ -the closest sound in the English language that is similar to this one would be the an in hang.

Example: main /mahn/ (hand), pain /pahn/ (bread)

/un/ and /um/ -to produce the nasal vowel sound, find the sound between /o/ and /e/.

Example: un /unh/ (one), brun /brunh/ (brown)

Practice pronouncing the following:

bain	banc	bond
sain	cent	son
daim	dans	don
fin	faon	fond
gain	gant	gond
geint	jean	jonc
lin	lent	long
main	ment	mont
pain	paon	pont
rein	rang	rond
thym	tant	ton
vin	vent	vont

Exercise

Here is a list of words that will let you practice most of the sounds in the French alphabet. Use a sound recorder and a free online application such as Google Translate to compare your pronunciation with that of a native speaker.

Consonant Sounds

- Beau
- Doux
- Fête
- Guerre
- Cabas
- Loup
- Femme
- Nous
- Agneaux
- Passé
- Roue
- Option
- Choux
- Tout
- Vous
- Hasard
- Joue

Semi-Vowel Sounds

- Travail
- Oui
- Huit

Vowel Sounds

- Là
- Pâte
- Aller
- Faite
- Maître
- Monsieur
- Régie
- Jeune
- Queue
- Haut
- Minimum
- Roue
- Sûr

Nasal Vowel Sounds

- Sans
- Pain
- Parfum
- Nom

Chapter 5: Numbers, Dates, and Time

How was your French pronunciation? Hope you did well so that you can move on to the next lesson, which is all about numbers. No, you do not have to solve mathematical problems in French, but you do need to know how to count and tell the date and time.

The French call their numbers "les chiffres", or "the figures". Just like English, French has two kinds of numbers, the cardinals (one, two), which are referred to as determiners, and the Ordinals (first, second), which are used as adjectives.

The Cardinals

Practice counting in French:

1: un

2: deux

3: trois

4: quatre

5: cinq

6: six

7: sept

8: huit

9: neuf

10: dix

11: onze

12: douze

13: treize

14: quatorze

15: quinze

16: seize

17: dix-sept

18: dix-huit

19: dix-neuf

20: vingt

21: vingt et un

22: vingt-deux

30: trente

31: trente et un

32: trente-deux

40: quarante

50: cinquante

60: soixante

70: soixante-dix

71: soixante et onze

72: souxante-douze

80: quatre-vingt

81: quatre-vingt-un

82: quatre-vingt-deux

90: quatre-vingt-dix

91: quatre-vingt-onze

100: cent

101: cent un

110: cent dix

200: deux cent

300: trois cent

1000: mille

In French, the "vergule" (comma) is used instead of the decimal point. For example, the English numbers "12.45" is written as "12,45" in French.

If you need to write numbers that are at least 4 digits, put a space in between instead of a comma. For instance, "3,200,000" becomes "3 200 000".

The Ordinals

To turn Cardinals into Ordinals, you simply add "ième". Only 1st different from the rest and is spelled as premier and written as 1er. However, 11th is 11e and spelled as "onzième", 21st is 21e and spelled as "vingt et unième", and so on.

The Months (Les Mois)

Unlike in the English language, the French do not capitalize the first letter of the months.

January: janvier

February: fevrier

March: mars

April: avril

May: mai

June: juin

July: juillet

August: août

September: septembre

October: octobre

November: novembre

December: décembre

The Days of the Week (Les Jours)

The same "no capitalization" rule applies to the days of the week. Keep in mind that they are all masculine, and that there is no need to use a preposition. For example, if you wish to say "On Wednesday..." in French, you simply say "Mercredi..."

Sunday: dimanche

Monday: lundi

Tuesday: mardi

Wednesday: mercredi

Thursday: jeudi

Friday: vendredi

Saturday: samedi

Here are some more useful words to help you with setting appointments:

Yesterday: hier

Today: aujourd'hui

Tomorrow: demain

Last week: cette semaine

This week: la semaine dernière

Next week: la semaine prochaine

To say the date in French, you start by saying the day, followed by the date (in the cardinal number), and then the month.

For example, you can say:

Demain c'est samedi, quatorze mars. ("Tomorrow is Saturday, 4th of March").

Telling the Time

"Heure" is the French word for the time, hour, or o'clock. It is pronounced as /urh/.

The French word for "quarter" is "quart" and "half" is "demi". Morning is "matin", Noon is "midi", Afternoon is "de l'après-midi", Night is "nuit", Evening is "soir", and Midnight is "minuit".

In French, this is what you usually say to ask for the time: "Quelle heure est-il?" /ke lur eh til/ ("What hour is it?")

Here are some sample sentences on how to tell the time:

➢ It is three o'clock: Il est trois heures.

➢ It is ten past three: Il est trois heures dix.

➢ It is a quarter past five: Il est cinq heures et quart.

➢ It is half past five: Il est cinq heures et demi.

➢ It is 12 noon: Il est midi.

➢ It is midnight: Il est minuit.

To state the difference between ante meridiem (a.m.) and post meridiem (p.m.) in French, you say du matin ("in the morning") or de l'après-midi ("in the afternoon"). Here are some examples:

➢ Six a.m: six heures du matin.

➢ 3:30 p.m.: trois heures et demi de l'après-midi.

You can also use military time or the 24-hour clock, such as "deux heures cinquante (2:50 a.m.) and vingt-quatre houres (12 midnight or 24:00).

Finally, the French write their time in this format: 1 h 10 (1:10 in English).

Exercise

1. Spell out the French cardinal numbers as far as you can go, then pronounce them and compare them to a recording you can find on a free online source.

2. Translate and write down the following into French, and then read them out loud:

- The 1st of January

- The 2nd of February

- The 3rd of March

- The 4th of April

- The 5th of May

- The 6th of June

- The 7th of July

- The 8th of August

- The 9th of September

- The 10th of October

- The 11th of November

- The 12th of December

3. Write down the time in words:

- 2 h 05
- 18 h 12
- 3 h 45
- 23 h 15
- 12 h
- 24 h
- 1 h 22
- 9 h 10
- 2 h 25
- 10 h 30
- 21 h 10
- 6 h 15

Chapter 6: Greetings and Other Useful Day to Day Phrases

The first thing that tourists and beginners usually turn to when it comes to learning a language quickly would be the greetings and commonly used phrases. This is actually a great way to start practicing French. Furthermore, it lets the learner take a peek into the culture of the French people. This chapter contains a large collection of greetings and phrases that you will find quite useful in everyday conversation.

Formal Greetings

Good day (Hello)	Bonjour!
Good morning	Bon matin!
Good afternoon	Bon après-midi!
Good evening	Bon soir!
Good night	Bon nuit!
How are you?	Comment allez-vous?
Very well, thank you.	Très bien, merci.
And you?	Et vous?
Goodbye (temporarily)	Au revoir.
Goodbye (permanently)	Adieu!
Bonne journée	(Have a) good day!

You can choose to say "bonjour" in the morning and in the afternoon. After 6 o'clock in the evening, you can say "bonsoir".

Informal Greetings

Hi!	Salut!
Is everything okay?	Tout va bien?
	Ça va?
Great!	Très bien!

Forms of Address

Mr.	(M) Monsieur, Messieurs
Mrs.	(Mme) Madame, Mesdames
Miss	(Mlle) Mademoiselle, Mesdemoiselles

Introductions

Formal: What is your name?	Comment vous appellez-vous?
Informal: What's your name?	Comment t'appelles-tu?
Quel est son prénom?	What is his/her first name?
My name is...	Je m'appelle...
Charmed.	Enchanté

Who is it?	Qui est-ce?
How old are you?	Quel âge avez-vous?
What is your nationality?	Quelle est vore nationalité?
Where do you live?	Où habitez-vous?
What do you do for a living?	Que faites-vous dans la vie?
Où travaillez-vous?	Where do you work?
What are your favorite hobbies?	Quels sont vos loisirs préférés?

Common Phrases

Pardon? Repeat that please. plaît.	Pardon? Répéte, s'il vous
I don't understand.	Je ne comprends pas.
I don't know.	Je ne sais pas.
Can you speak slower, please? lentement, s'il vous plaît?	Pouvez-vous parler plus
Excuse me.	Excusez-moi.
(If you) please.	S'il vous plaît.

Un moment, s'il vous plaît.	One moment, please.
I am sorry.	Je suis désolé/désolée.
That's okay!	Ce n'est pas grave!
Thank you very much!	Merci beaucoup.
You are welcome	Je vous en prie
It's nothing.	De rien.
	Pas de quoi.

Key Question Words

It is imperative to know these key question words when asking for specific information:

How many...	Combien de...
How much...	Combien
At what time...	À quelle heure
How...	Comment
Where...	Où
Why...	Pourqui
What...	Qu'est-ce que
When...	Quand
Who...	Qui...
Which.../ What...	Quel(s)/Quelle(s)

Talking about Directions and Places

"Where is...?" is a question that you need to master in French when you are traveling. Here are some common phrases:

Where is the Eiffel Tower?	Où est la tour Eiffel?
Where is the bathroom?	Où sont les toilettes?
Where is the bus going?	Où va ce bus?
Where does this road lead?	Où mène cette rue?

To say that you are going to or that you are staying in a particular place, use the preposition "à".

For example, if you are going to say "I am going to Paris", say: Je vais à Paris." On the other hand, "we are in Paris," translates to "Nous sommes à Paris."

If you want to talk about staying at or going to places in general (such as museums and cathedrals), you should add the definite article after "à". For example:

Pierre is going to the museum.

Pierre va au musée.

Sarah wants to go to the cathedral.

Sarah veut aller à la cathédrale.

Go to the coffee shop.

Aller au café.

To say that the place is within eyesight, you can use these phrases:

Question: Où est le bâtiment? (Where is the building?)/ Où sont les bâtiments? (Where are the buildings?)

Answer: Le voici! (Here it is!) or La voilà! (There it is!)/ Les voilà! (There they are!)

Talking about the Weather

"Le temps" is the French word for the weather. It is often a favorite topic among native French speakers, particularly if the weather is bad.

In French, the names of the seasons are:

Spring   le printemps

Summer   le été

Fall   l'automne

Winter   l'hiver

To ask "What is the weather like?", say: Quel temp fait-il?

To answer, say: Il fait... and then describe it as:

Warm   Chaud

Cold   Froid

Nice   Beau

Doux   Mild

Frais   Cool

Mauvais   Bad

Du soleil   Sunny

Du vent   Windy

If it is raining, say: Il pleut.

If it is snowing, say: Il neige.

To talk about the temperature, you say: La température est de vingt cinq degrés. (It is 25 degrees [Celsius]).

Talking about Where you Live

"Habiter" is the French word for living in a space, while "vivre" refers to both time and space.

For instance, if you say "they lived in the 19th century", you make use of "vivre", hence: "ils vivaient dans le dix-neufième siècle." Keep in mind that vivre is an irregular verb.

If you wish to talk about where you live, you use "habiter", such as:

J'habite danse une appartement. (I live in an apartment.)

Nous habitons une maison. (We live in a house.)

Exercise

Practice saying the French counterpart of these greetings and phrases without looking at the notes:

- Good day (Hello)
- Good morning
- Good afternoon
- Good evening
- Good night
- How are you?
- Very well, thank you.
- And you?
- Goodbye (temporarily)
- Goodbye (permanently)
- Bonne journée
- Hi!
- Is everything okay?
- Great!
- Formal: What is your name?
- Informal: What's your name?
- Quel est son prénom?
- My name is...

- Charmed.
- Who is it?
- How old are you?
- What is your nationality?
- Where do you live?
- What do you do for a living?
- Où travaillez-vous?
- What are your favorite hobbies?
- Pardon? Repeat that please.
- I don't understand.
- I don't know.
- Can you speak more slowly, please?
- Excuse me.
- (If you) please.
- Un moment, s'il vous plaît.
- I am sorry.
- That's okay!
- Thank you very much!
- You are welcome
- It's nothing.

Chapter 7: Gender and Articles

Gender and articles in the French language go hand in hand, because they are dependent on each other throughout the communication process. Take note that each noun in the French language has a gender: masculine or feminine.

Gender

The nouns were determined to be masculine or feminine not by how "male" or "female" they are (except in the case of the sex of most living things, such as the rooster and the hen), but by how the word is pronounced, spelled, and how it was developed.

There is no exact "formula" to determine whether a noun is masculine or feminine, and the only way to become familiar with this is to constantly expose yourself to as much French input as possible. Upon encountering a noun, you must also memorize its gender.

Persons

When a noun represents a person, the sex of the person determines the gender (but keep in mind that there are still exceptions to this "rule"). Generally, the female form of the noun is created by placing an -e to a masculine noun. For example:

Tony is a student.   Tony est un étudiant.

Sarah is a student.   Sarah est une étudiante.

If a masculine noun already ends with an -e, there is no need to add another -e to make it feminine. The noun, therefore, can be applicable to both. For example:

Benedict is a poet.

Jane is a poet.

Benedict est poète.

Jane est poète.

Animals

The masculinity or femininity of the French nouns for animals is not always based on the animal's gender. For instance, snails are often "masculine", because the French always refer to them as "un escargot" regardless as to whether it is a male or female snale. On the other hand, ants are always "la fourmi" even if there also girl and boy ants.

Take note that many animals in the French language are irregular masculine and feminine forms. For example:

Male lion: le lion

Female lion: la lionne

Male dog: le chien

Female dog: la chienne

Ideas and Objects

Nouns that represent abstractions and nonliving things are arbitrary, although in general you can infer their gender based on the ending of the word.

In general, nouns ending in -aire, -age, -é, -et, -ien, -in, -nt, - le, -eau, -asme, and -isme are masculine.

For example:

-aire: un dictionnaire (a dictionary), le proriétaire (the owner)

-age: un sondage (a survey), le reportage (the report)

-é: un café (a coffee shop), le cité (the city)

-et: un billet (a ticket), le sujet (the subject)

-ien: un magicien (a magician), le musicien (the musician)

-in: un bain (a bath), le cousin (the cousin)

-nt: un accident (an accident), le monument (the monument)

-le: un vignoble (a vineyard), le diable (the devil)

-eau: un bateau (a boat), le bureau (the office)

-asme and -isme: le sarcasme (sarcasm), le romantisme (romanticism), le optimisme (optimism)

Generally speaking, nouns ending in -ade, -aison, -té, -ette, -ance/ -ence,
-ve,
-ure, -ille/ -elle are feminine. For example:

-ade: une salade (a salad), la limonade (the lemonade)

-aison: une raison (a reason), la saison (the season)

-té: la liberté (liberty), la beauté (beauty)

-ette: une fourchette (the fork), la baguette (the baguette)

-ance and -ence: la resistance (the resistance), la conférence (the conference)

-ve: la larve (the larva), la lessive (the washing)

-ure: une coiffure (a hairstyle), la blessure (the injury)

-ille and -elle: la veille (vigil), la bouteille (the bottle), la dentelle (lace), la vaisselle (the dishes)

Determining the gender of the nouns in French is imperative since all modifiers should agree in it. For instance, the forms of adjectives and past participles should be based on whether a noun is masculine or feminine. For example:

A white dog. (the French noun "dog" is masculine)   Un chien blanc.

A white car. ("car" is feminine in French)   Une voiture blanche.

A cold morning. ("morning" is masculine in French)   Un matin froid.

A cold night. (in French, "night" is feminine)   Une nuite froide.

The Articles

In the English language, the articles are "a", "an", and "the". In French, articles play a major role in communication, for it is not possible to use a noun alone.

The articles in French are classified as either definite or indefinite, which is same as in English. One major difference is that French articles characterize the masculinity or femininity of the noun that it precedes. It is therefore wise to memorize not just nouns, but also the articles that accompany them.

The Indefinite Articles

An indefinite article is a determiner that pertains to a nonspecific reference. The indefinite articles in English are "a", "an", and "some". In French, they are "un", "une", and "des", respectively.

"Un" is used for masculine nouns. For example:

A cat (male)	Un chat
A telephone	Un téléphone
A knife	Un couteau

"Une" is used for feminine nouns. For example:

A cat (female)	Une chatte
A television	Une télévision
A fork	Une fourchette

"Des" is used for plural nouns. For example:

Some tomatoes	Des onions
Some sausages	Des saucisses

To talk about multiple nouns you have to repeat the indefinite article before every noun. For example:

Un couteau et une fourchette. (A knife and a fork.)

The Definite Articles

A definite article is a determiner that is used to indicate a specific or certain noun or to refer to a noun that has already been mentioned or specified. "The" is the English definite article. In French, these are "le", "la", "l' ", and "les".

"Le" is placed before a masculine singular noun that begins with a consonant. For example:

The cheese	Le fromage
The rooster	Le coq
The dictionary	Le dictionnaire

"La" is placed before a feminine singular noun that begins with a consonant. For example:

The lemonade	La limonade
The hen	La poule
The philosophy	La philosophie

"L'" is placed before a singular noun that begins with a vowel or with a silent "h". It is the contracted form of "le" and "la". For example:

The man	L'homme
The school	L'école
The hospital	L'hôpital

"Les" is placed before plural nouns. It does not have a contracted form. If it precedes a word that begins with a vowel sound or a silent "h", the "s" in "les" (which is usually silent), is pronounced with a /z/ sound. For example:

The men	Les hommes
The hens	Les poules
The hospitals	Les hôpitaux

To talk about multiple nouns you have to repeat the definite article before every noun. For example:

Acheter le sac bleu et les chaussures noires. (Buy the blue book and the black shoes.)

The Partitive Articles

A partitive article refers to only a part of the object and not the object as a whole. It is used whenever the exact amount of an item cannot be determined. In English, they are "any" and "some". Often, they can be omitted; you will still be understood if you choose to say either "He has water" or "He has some water".

However, these articles cannot be omitted in the French language. Every time you encounter a situation wherein "some" or "any" is needed in the sentence, you must use them.

For masculine singular nouns, "du" is used. For example:

I have (some) paper.   Je ai du papier.

For feminine singular nouns, "de la" is used. For example:

Do you have (any) lemonade?   Avez-vous de la limonade?

For singular nouns that begin with a vowel or a silent "h", "de l'" is used. For example:

She has (some) water?   Elle a de l'eau?

For plural nouns, "des" is used. For example:

There are children in the park.   Il ya des enfants dans le parc.

Exercise

1. State the correct article before each French noun:

- _chanteur
- _étudiant
- _avenue
- _prénom
- _boulivard
- _vocabulaire
- _maison
- _vacance
- _vin
- _argent
- _chapeau
- _espoir
- _fraise
- _boisson
- _prison

2. Rewrite the following nouns in the feminine form:

- Acteur
- Chat
- Neveu

- Mari
- Chanteur

3. Rewrite the following nouns in the masculine form:

- Vraie
- Belle
- Vieille
- Bleue
- Curieuse

Chapter 8: Nouns and Pronouns

The French call the noun "nom", which is also the same word for "name". After all, nouns are used to give names to people, animals, places, things, ideas, events, and so on.

French nouns, just like English nouns, are characterized as either common or proper, singular or plural, and count or mass. The major difference is that French nouns have a gender, which will be discussed in detail in the next chapter.

Common and Proper Nouns

A common noun is a generic term for all the members of a class of words. The first letter of the word is never capitalized. For example: a cat is "un chat".

A proper noun is a term that denotes a specific thing, and the first letter of the word is always capitalized. For example: Benedict and Jane is "Benedict et Jane".

Singular and Plural Nouns

As you know, singular denotes "one" and plural denotes "more than one". In French, as in English, you add an -s at the end of a singular noun to make it plural. For example: le chat (the cat) becomes les chats (the cats). Take note that you can also use the indefinite article "des", such as by saying "des chats".

However, French singular nouns that end in -s, -x, and -z do not need to be changed to turn them into the plural form. Instead, the article before it is changed. For example: le bras (the arm) becomes les bras (the arms), croix (the cross) becomes les croix (the crosses), and le nez (the nose) becomes les nez (the noses).

Generally, for French singular nouns that end in -eu, -eau, and -ou, an -x is attached to the end to turn them into plural form. For example: le bateau (the boat) becomes les bateaux (the boats), le cheveu (the hair) becomes les cheveux (the hairs). Keep in mind that there are exceptions, such as le cou (the neck), which becomes les cous (the necks).

French singular nouns that end in -ail, and -al can be pluralized by replacing them with -aux. For example: l'animal (the animal) becomes les animaux (the animals), and un travail (the job) becomes des travaux (the jobs). Again, there are exceptions, such as un carnival (a carnival) to des carnivals (the carnivals), and un chandail (a sweater) to des chandails (the sweaters).

Plural Masculine Form for Adjectives

You do not have to change the masculine plural form of adjectives that have -s or -x at the end. For example: un cheveu gris (a gray hair) to des cheveux gris (the gray hairs).

However, for masculine plural form of adjectives that have -al or -eau at the end, you will need to change them to -aux or -eux, respectively. For example: le beau bateau (the beautiful boat) to les beaux bateaux (the beautiful boats).

Subject Pronouns

A sentence should always have a subject that does something and a verb to show what that subject is doing. There are 3 types of subjects, namely the 1st person, 2nd person, and the 3rd person.

In English, the singular forms are "I", "You", and "He" or "She", respectively. In French, these are "Je", "Tu" or "Vous" and "Il" or "Elle".

The plural forms in English are "We", "You", and "They", while in French, these are "Nous" or "On", "Vous", and "Ils" or "Elles".

➢ Je (I) becomes J' if it is followed by a vowel sound or a silent "h". For example: J'habite à Paris. (I live in Paris).

➢ You use "tu" (you) when you are talking to your friends, to children, or to close family members. For example: Tu es Sarah? (Are you Sarah?). "Vous" is used in a formal conversation. For example: Vous voulez? (Do you want (it)?)

➢ "Il" and "Elle" are French for "He" and "She" respectively. For example: Il mange le gâteau et elle boit du thé. (He is eating cake and she is drinking tea).

➢ Nous is the French pronoun for "we". For example: Nous aimons ce vin. (We like this wine). The more colloquial pronoun for "we" is "on". For example: On habite ici (We live here).

➢ "Ils" and "Elles" are used for plural masculine and feminine subjects, respectively. For example: Ils sont en amour avec elle (They (the men) are in love with her). Elles aiment regarder des films romantiques (They (the women) love to watch romantic movies).

➢ In situations wherein all of the members of a group are not female (such as a group having two men and three women), or if you do not know the sex of the members of the group, then "ils" is used.

➢ Familiarize yourself with the inflection of verbs (called "Conjugation") depending on the subject. Here is an example:

Infinitive (or base form): habiter (to live in)

Subject Pronouns and Conjugation:

Je	habite
Tu	habites
Il, Elle	habite
Nous	mangeons
Vous	mangez
Ils, Elles	mangent

Exercise

1. Turn these singular nouns into plural, including the proper article before each.

- Tante (f)
- Vélo (m)
- Chamber (f)
- Tatou (m)
- Livre (m)
- Voiture (f)
- Bijou (m)
- Boisson (f)
- Enfant (m)
- Chaise (f)
- Cheval (m)
- Soeur (f)
- L'arbre (m)
- Pou (m)

2. Translate these English sentences into French, following the proper subject pronouns. You may use a dictionary to help guide you in verb conjugations:

- I live in the United States.
- I am American.

- He eats at that restaurant.

- She does not like the food.

- They are singing a Christmas song.

- *(While talking to your cousin):* You are beautiful!

- *(While talking to a stranger):* You are good at drawing.

Chapter 9: Adjectives and Adverbs

To create meaningful phrases in the French language, it is important to know how to describe the nouns and verbs using adjectives and adverbs.

Adjectives

An adjective is a word that is used to modify (or describe) a noun. The ending of a French adjective is modified based on the number and gender of the noun. Here are the basic grammar rules for French adjectives:

> To turn most masculine adjectives into the feminine form, simply add an -e at the end of the word. For example: intelligent becomes intelligente, mauvais becomes mauvaise (bad), and bleu becomes bleue (blue).

> If the masculine adjective already has an -e at the end of the word, you no longer have to add another -e to make it feminine. For example: riche (rich), calme (calm), and utile (useful) are applicable to both masculine and feminine nouns.

> The masculine adjectives that have -er at the end, you will need to change it to -ère to turn it into a feminine form. For example: premier becomes première (first), and dernier becomes dernière (last).

> If a masculine adjective ends in -f, you modify it into the feminine form by changing the -f into a -ve. For example: neuf becomes neuve (new), and actif becomes active (busy).

- To modify the masculine adjectives that end in -eur into the feminine form, there are three patterns: by adding an -e, modifying -eur into -euse (if it is derived from a verb), and if it is -teur it is changed into -trice. For example: majeur becomes majeure (major), moqueur becomes moqueuse (mocking), and protecteur becomes protectrice (protective).

- For masculine adjectives that end in -x, the -x is removed and replaced with -se to modify it into the feminine form. For example: heureux becomes heureuse (happy).

- If a masculine adjective ends in -et, change it to ète to modify it into the feminine form. For example: concret becomes concrète (concrete).

- For masculine adjectives that end in a single consonant, double the final consonant and add -e. For example: cruel becomes cruelle (cruel), and bon becomes bonne (good).

- If a masculine adjectives ends in -gu, an -ë is added in the end to modify it into the feminine form. For example: ambigu becomes ambiguë (ambiguous).

- Remember that there are irregular adjectives in the French language, where the masculine form is completely different from the feminine form. For example: beau is to belle (handsome or beautiful), mou is to molle (soft).

An important rule to remember in the French language is the placement of an adjective. Contrary to English rules, you are supposed to place a French adjective after the noun if you want to express it in the literal sense.

Here are some examples: une table carrée (a square table), une robe bleue (a blue dress)

French adjectives that are placed before a noun are those that fall under the following descriptors: beauty, age, good and bad, and size (exception: grand).

Here are some examples: une belle maison (a beautiful house), un vieil homme (an old man), un mauvais parent (a bad parent), and un petit biscuit (a small cookie).

Non-descriptive adjectives (demonstrative, indefinite, negative, interrogative, possessive) are also placed before the noun.

For example: ces sacs (these bags), chaque femme (each woman), quel livre? (which book?), mon mari (my husband).

Certain adjectives can have either a figurative or analytic (literal) meaning, enabling you to place them before a noun if the meaning is figurative, and after the noun if the meaning is analytic.

Here are some examples:

Une grande femme (a great woman) large woman) | Une femme grande (a

Un triste enfant (a bad child) child) | Un enfant triste (a sad

Adverbs

An adverb is a word that is used to describe the manner in which something happens or occurs. It is used to modify verbs, adjectives, and other adverbs.

In English, and adverb is formed by placing -ly to the end of the adjective. As for most French adverbs, you do so by placing -ment to the end of the feminine form of adjective. You also add -ment to adjectives that end in -u and -i. If the adjective ends in "t" you usually drop the "t" and add the -mment.

For example: absolu becomes absolument (absolutely), vrai becomes vraiment (truly), and patient becomes patiemment (patiently).

If an adjective ends in -ant, you turn it into an adverb by changing it to -amment. If it ends in -ent, it should become -emment.

The natural position of a French adverb is right after the verb. However, if you wish to express an adverb in terms of place, time, frequency, and manner, there are three positions for the adverb: at the beginning of the sentence, right before the subject, or at the end of the sentence.

Exercise

Modify these adjectives from the masculine form to the feminine form. After that, practice using them with French nouns:

- Américain
- Noir
- Brun
- Occupé
- Froid
- Anglais
- Faux
- Français
- Vert
- Chaud
- Moyen
- Étroit
- Violet
- Petit
- Vrai
- Blanc

Modify these adjectives from masculine to feminine forms, then into adverbs:

- Franc

- Parfait

- Haute

- Particulier

- Spécial

Chapter 10: Demonstratives

Demonstratives are used with nouns to clearly show or demonstrate specific items. The demonstrative adjectives in the English language, for instance, are "this", "that", "these", and "those".

Demonstrative Adjectives

The French counterparts of "this" and "that" are are "ce" and "cet" for masculine, and "cette" for feminine. Here are some examples:

> Cette fenêtre est grande. (This/ That window is large).

> Ce garçon est âgé de neuf ans. (This boy is nine years old).

If "ce" is followed by a word that starts with a vowel or a silent "h", it becomes "cet". Always remember that you do not contract "ce", and the c' expression in "c'est" is not referred to as a demonstrative adjective. Rather, it is an indefinite demonstrative pronoun. Here is an example:

> Qui est cet homme? (Who is that man?).

The counterparts for "these" and "those" are "ces" for both masculine and feminine. Here is an example:

> Je aime ces fauteuils. (I like these/ those armchairs).

Keep in mind that the demonstrative adjective is always repeated before every noun. For example:

> Elle aimerait essayer cette robe et ces pantalons. (She would like to try this dress and these pants).

In order to distinguish between this/ these from that/those, you add -ci at the end of the noun after this/ these, and you add -là at the end of the noun after that/ those. For example:

Cet étudiant-ci mange trop. (This student eats too much).

Cette femme-là regarde faim. (That woman looks hungry).

Ces livres-ci sont vieux. (These books are old).

Ces chaussures-là sont mignons. (Those shoes are cute).

Demonstrative Pronouns

Demonstrative pronouns in the English language are "this one" and "that one". For example: "It's easy." and "that's true".

The masculine singular demonstrative pronouns are "celui", and the plural is "ceux". The feminine singular demonstrative nouns are "celle", and the plural is "celles".

Remember that you should not use demonstrative pronouns on their own, because they need to be used with a suffix, in a prepositional phrase, and followed by a relative pronoun and dependent clause.

To recognize the difference between "this one" and "that one", you also add -ci and là, respectively, right next to the pronoun. Here are some examples:

Quelle robe que vous aimez mieux, celui-ci ou celui-là? (Which dress do you like better, this one or that one?)

Je veux essayer ceux-ci et ceux-là. (I want to try these and those)

In prepositional phrases, you use "de" to distinguish the origin or possession. For example:

Quel est le gâteau sucré? Celui de Sarah ou celui de Louis? (Which cake tastes sweeter? The one from Sarah or the one from Louis?)

Here is an example if the demonstrative pronoun is followed by a relative pronoun plus a dependent clause:

Ceux qui ont du talent peuvent participer au concours. (Those who are talented can join the contest).

Exercise

1. Translate the following sentences into French.

- Is this coat made of leather?

- She is going to drink that beer.

- I do not like those pictures.

- That restaurant is popular.

- These sandwiches are delicious!

- They want to buy this computer.

- Please iron this shirt for me.

- Those dogs belong to Peter.

- I think these flowers are beautiful.

- Can I borrow that table?

2. Fill in the blanks using celui, celle, ceux, or celles.

- ___avec les cheveux courts , vous voyez ? ce est ma fille.

- De ces trois lampes , je préfère___.

- ___qui veulent regarder le film devrait aider à nettoyer cette salle .

- Parmi ces livres, ___de Paris est le plus romantique.

- Il y a de nombreuses pistes de ski en Canada. ___ de la Colombie-Britannique sont les plus actifs.

Chapter 11: Possessives

Possessives, in general, express a relation of possession. They are used to express a relationship between objects and persons. Possessives are usually placed before a noun or before a pronoun. For instance, the possessive adjectives in English are "my", "your", "his/ her/ its", "our", "your", and "their".

Possessive Adjectives

In French, the singular form of possessive adjectives adapt to the gender of the noun. But for their plural form, there is no distinction in gender.

The French masculine form of "my" is "mon" and the feminine is "ma". For the plural, it is "mes". For example:

Mon chat est âgé. (My cat is old).

Ma fenêtre est ouverte. (My window is open).

Tous mes chiens sont daschunds. (All my dogs are daschunds).

The French masculine form of "your" is "ton" and the feminine is "ta". For the plural, it is "tes". For example:

Ton ville est belle. (Your city is beautiful).

Ta maison est magnifique. (Your house is magnificent).

Tes cookies goût délicieux. (Your cookies taste delicious).

The French form of "his" is "son" while for "her" it is "sa". For the plural, it is "ses". For example:

Son voiture est nouvelle. (His car is new).

Sa jupe est courte. (Her skirt is short).

Ses dents sont trop blanc. (His teeth are too white).

Take note that for feminine nouns that begin with a vowel or a silent "h", "mon", "ton", and "son" are used instead of "ma", "ta", and "sa".

For example: amie (feminine) is "mon amie" (my girl friend), histoire (feminine) is "ton histoire" (your story), and "plume" (feminine) is "son autre plume" (his/her other pen).

Also, "son", "sa", and "ses" are only identified based on the context which is meant. It typically refers to the possessed rather than the possessor.

For example: "Anna a son chemise." (Anna has her shirt), and "Chaque homme a ses problèmes." (Every man has his problems).

The French form of "our" is "notre" for either masculine or feminine. In the mixed plural form, it is "nos". For example:

Notre fille joue du piano. (Our daughter plays the piano).

Nos chansons sont écrites en anglais. (Our songs are written in English).

The French form of the plural "your" is "votre" for either masculine or feminine. For the plural form, it is "vos". For example:

Tout le monde , rappelez-vous ceci: votre travail est de faire attention. (Everyone, remember this: your job is to pay attention).

Chacun d'entre vous doit écouter attentivement. Vos enfants sont votre seule responsabilité. (Each of you must listen carefully. Your children are your responsibility.)

The French form of "their" is "leur" for either masculine or feminine. For the plural, it is "leurs". For example:

Leur grand-père est triste. (Their grandfather is sad).

Leurs chaussures sont sales. (Their shoes are dirty).

Possessive Pronouns

A possessive pronoun is a word used to replace a noun that is modified by a possessive adjective. In English, the possessive pronouns are "mine", "yours", "his", "hers", "ours", and "theirs".

The French masculine singular form of "mine" is "le mien" and the feminine is "la mienne". The plural masculine is "les miens" and the plural feminine is "les miennes".

The French masculine singular form of "yours" is "le tien" and the feminine is "la tienne". Thep lural masculine is "les tiens" and the plural feminine is "les tiennes:.

The French masculine singular form of "his, hers" is "le sien" and the feminine is "la sienne". Thep lural masculine is "les siens" and the plural feminine is "les siennes".

The French masculine singular form of "ours" is "le notre" and the feminine is "la notre". The plural masculine and feminine is "les notres".

The French masculine form of the plural "yours" for singular is "le votre" and the feminine is "la votre". The masculine and feminine for the plural is "les votres".

The French masculine form of "theirs" for the singular is "le leur" and the feminine is "la leur". The masculine and feminine for the plural is "les leurs".

Notice that they agree in both the gender and the number with the noun denoting the object possessed. For example:

Je vois ton fille, mais la mienne n'est past encore arrivé.

(I see your daughter, but mine has not arrived yet).

When "à" (the preposition "to") or "de" (the preposition "from") goes before the possessive pronoun, you need to contract the preposition with the definite article. For example:

Vous parlez à ton oncle. Je vais parler au mien.

(You talk to your uncle, I will talk to mine).

Exercise

1. Transform the following into plural form. For example: "Donnez-lui sa robe" becomes "Donnez-lui ses robes".

● J'ai lu ta livre.

● Mon portefeuille est en lambeaux.

● Votre tante ne nous a pas aidé.

● Sa peinture est laid.

● Ton employé est têtue.

2. Translate the following into French, then change them into possessive pronouns:

● My brothers.

● Their daughters.

● His notebooks.

● Her apartment.

● Her mother and father.

● Your ideas.

● Their table.

Chapter 12: Interrogatives

An interrogative is a sentence of inquiry which seeks a reply. In the French language, there are four ways to form interrogatives:

One way is by using "Est-ce que" (pronounces as /es khe/), which literally translates to "is it that". You can place it at the start of an affirmative sentence so that you can turn that sentence into a question.

Another way to use "est-ce que" is for you to put a question word before it (remember "key question words" from Chapter 6?).

To ask formal questions, what you can do is invert the conjugated verb and subject pronoun, then join them together with a hyphen.

Keep in mind that when you are using the inversion method with the 3rd person singular (il, elle, on), and a verb that ends in a vowel, you need to put a -t- in between the verb and the subject pronoun.

You can also use inversion if you want to form negative questions. It is also good to remembet that when you reply in the affirmative to a negative question, do not use "oui"; instead, use "si".

The third way to form interrogatives is to simply change the intonation of your voice by raising it at the end. This is a very casual way of asking questions, though.

Lastly, if you want to ask a question to which the answer is most likely "yes", then state an affirmative sentence and then add "n'est-ce pas?" at the end.

Here are some common questions that you can memorize to practice asking questions in French:

Where is terminal 2/ gate 2?	Où se trouve le terminal 2/ la porte 2?
Where is the check-in counter?	Où dois-je enregistrer mes baggages?
Do you have your boarding card?	Avez-vous votre carte d'embarquement?
Where is the baggage reclaim counter?	Où dois-je aller recuperer mes baggages?
How much is this?	Combien ca coute?
Can we see the menu?	Pouvons-nous voir la carte?

Exercise

Turn the following statements into questions, alternating the four different methods per item:

- Ils ont une nouvelle maison.

- Vous avez commencé en retard.

- Elle a une bonne carrière.

- Vous allez boire ce jus.

- Colleen arrive pour faire son travail.

- Elle vient de regarder le film.

- Nous voyageons souvent.

- M. Du Mont va se lever tot.

Chapter 13: Negation

It is quite easy to make negative sentences in the French language. You simply need to put "ne... pas" on either side of the verb. All other components of the sentence remain the same.

For example:

Je bois du café. (I drink coffee)

Je ne bois pas de café (I don't drink coffee)

Just remember that if the verb begins with a vowel or a silent "h", then "n'... pas" is used instead.

In colloquial French, the speakers often omit the "ne". Also, the "ne" is solely used in sentences that contain a verb. If a sentence that does not have a verb, the negative word is used by itself.

For example:

Ce n'est pas vrai (It's not true) is transformed into C'est pas vrai.

Je ne crois pas (I don't believe it) is transformed into Je crois pas.

Aside from "pas", you can choose to use other expressions of negation after "ne", namely:

non

This is usually used as a negative response to a question.

For example:

Marc: Est-il chez lui? (is he at home?)

Sonja: Non, il est au supermarché. (No, he is at the supermarket)

ne.. plus ("no longer")

This is the negative of encore (yet) and toujours (always).

For example:

Il a décidé de ne plus boire de l'alcool. (He decided not to drink alcohol)

ne... pas encore ("not yet")

This is the negation of déjà (already).

For example:

Benedict: Jane a arrivé? (Has Jane arrived?)

Nadine: Non, pas encore. (No, not yet).

ne... personne (no one)

For example:

Ils ne connaissent personne. (They don't know anyone)

ne... jamais (never)

This is the negation of toujours (always), quelquefois (sometimes), souvent (often), and parfois (occasionally).

For example:

Marsha: Pensez-vous aller à l'église le dimanche? (Do you go to church on Sundays?)

Mia: Non, je n'y vais jamais. (No, I never go there)

ne... ni... ni... ("neither... nor")

This is the negative form of et (and) and ou (or).

For example:

Je ne ai ni le chocolat, ni comme la vanille. (I neither like chocolate nor vanilla).

ne... rien (nothing)

Non merci, je ne ai pas besoin de rien. (No thank you, I don't need anything)

que (only)

Je ne ai que de l'eau. (I only have water).

Exercise

Change the following statements into the negative form.

- Je vais souvent au Canada.

- Nous marchons ensemble tout le tim.

- Je suis encore faim.

- Elle a déjà une voiture.

- Il veut se baigner ici toujours.

- Elle a beaucoup des enfants.

- Jon Snow sait tout.

- Les étudiants ont la classe.

- Je peux parler français et en allemand.

- Je aime aller à la plage tous les étés.

Chapter 14: Prepositions

A preposition is a function word or a group of words that is made to connect one component of the sentence to another. In general, it indicates the relation of the meaning that unites these components.

For instance, in the French language, the components are: possession or "de", and place or "dance" and "en face de". Sometimes, a preposition is simply a tool that has no specific meaning, such as "à". A preposition needs to precede a noun.

"de" is the French counterpart of the English "from" and "à" is that of "to". They are used with verbs to express a movement. Aller à means "to go to" and Venir de means "to come from".

To be more specific, de and à are used to refer to locations - not the movements themselves. "De" signifies that source of the movement while "à" refers to the destination. This can be observed in the following example: "d'ici à là" (an expression which means from here to there), d'ici being the contraction of de ici, ici meaning "here", and là meaning "there".

Take note that the meanings of "de" and "à" change either depending on the verb to which they are associated or on their role in a certain sentence.

"De" can mean the following: source, purpose, possession, destination, quantity, measure, cause, material, or point of departure. This preposition also contracts whenever it is used with a definite article. With the article "le" it becomes "du", with the article "la" it becomes "de la", with the article "l'" it becomes "de l'", and with the article "les" it becomes "des".

"À" refers to characteristic or purpose. This preposition is highly versatile and can mean a lot of things, such as "at", "in", "of", "to", and "by", depending to the noun to which it is associated. The following are the different functions of à: time, location or destination, possession, distance, and to describe a particular action/ weight and measure/ function or purpose.

This preposition also contracts whenever it is used with a definite article. With the article "le" it becomes "au", with the article "la" it becomes "à la", with "l'" it becomes "à l'", and with "les" it becomes "aux".

Other Prepositions

Here is a list of the other prepositions in the French language.

next to, beside	à côté de
After	après
about, on the subject of	au sujet de
Before	avant
With	avec
at the home/office of, among	chez
Against	contre
In	dans
according to	d'après
from, of, about	de
since, for	depuis
in back of, behind	derrière
in front of	devant
during, while	durant
in, on, to	en
outside of	en dehors de
facing, across from	en face de
Between	entre
Toward	envers

Approximately	environ
outside of	hors de
until, up to, even	jusque
far from	loin de
Despite	malgré
by, through	par
Among	parmi
During	pendant
For	pour
Near	près de
as for, regarding	quant à
Without	sans
according to	Selon
Under	sous
according to	suivant
On	sur
Toward	vers

Exercise

Provide the proper preposition in the blanks:

- Le week-end , ils aiment aller _théâtre.

- Est- ce que vous voulez venir _parti?

- Elle habite _France, _Paris.

- La maison _Jaques est grande.

- Ce est l'ordinateur portable _ médecin?

- Voir le tableau _ étudiants.

- Le vélo _Beatrice est très ancienne.

- Ce est l' histoire _friend de Fiona.

- Ces chaussures ne sont pas _cuir, qu'ils sont _plastique.

Chapter 15: Comparisons

Comparisons are words that are used to compare things. In English, the comparative forms make use of "as (adjective/ adverb) as", and "is/ are (adjective/ adverb) than". Take note that "que" or "q'" is the French word for "than".

Regular Comparative Forms

In French, what signifies the comparative forms with adverbs and adjectives are:

For more than: "plus", followed by the adverb or adjective, then "que/ "q'"

For example: Sam est plus jeune que Simon. (Sam is younger than Simon).

For equal to: "aussi, followed by the adverb or adjective, then "que/ q'"

For example: Marsha est aussi jolie que Nadine. (Marsha is as pretty as Nadine).

For less than: "moins, followed by the adverb or adjective, then "que/ q'"

For example: Michael est moins riche que David. (Michael is less rich than David).

The comparative forms with nouns are:

For more than: "plus", followed by "de/ d'", noun, then "que/ "qu'"

For example: Nous avons plus de nourriture que lui. (We have more food than her).

For equal to: "autant", followed by "de/ d'", noun, then "que/ "qu'"

For example: Il ya juste autant de lait dans son verre que le vôtre . (There is just as much milk in her glass as yours.)

For less than: "moins", followed by "de/ d'", noun, then "que/ "qu'"

For example: Il ya moins de personnes au centre commercial que dans le supermarché. (There are less people at the mall than at the supermarket).

Irregular Comparative Forms

Adjectives

"Bon" et "Mauvais" (Good and Bad)

Bon: Meilleur (better), followed by the adjective, followed by "que/ q'"

Mauvais: plus mauvais (badder), followed by the adjective, followed by "que/ q'"

Pire (worse), followed by the adjective, followed by "que/ q'"

For example: Ses écriture est pire qu'avant. (Her handwriting is worse than before).

Adverbs

Bien (good): mieux que (better than)

For example: L'équipe bleue joue mieux que l'équipe rouge. (The blue team plays better than the red team).

Superlatives

This is the superlative comparative form:

Le/ La/ Les plus (the most), followed by the adjective/ adverb, then by "de"

For example: Elle est le chef le plus talentueux de France. (She is the most talented chef in France).

Le/ La/ Les moins (the least), followed by the adjective/ adverb, then by "de"

For example: Il est le moins de succès parmi les frères. (He is the least successful among the brothers).

Le/ La/ Les plus/ de moins de, followed by the noun

For example: Ce est le plus de passagers numériques que je ai jamais vu. (This is the most number of passengers I have ever seen).

Verb, followed by le plus/ le moins

For example: C'est Andrea qui travaille le plus. (It is Andrea who works the most).

"Comme" (Such as): adjective, followed by "comme". If "aussi" or "si" is removed, "comme" is used in its place.

For example: Il est beau comme une célébrité. (He is as handsome as a celebrity).

Exercise

1. Compare the following:

- Jaque's height: 1,70 m, Pierre's height: 1,80 m

- Troy's weight: 80 kg, Austin's weight: 90 kg

- Paris et Thaïlande (use the following adjectives: grand, intéressant, cher)

- Le vélo et le Revo (use the following adjectives: rapide, joli, cher, comfortable)

2. Fill in the blanks:

- Sylvie est paresseuse. Tabitha est travailleuse. Sylvie travailé _Tabitha.

- Colleen est rapide. Elena est lente. Colleen court _Elena.

- Philippe est timid. Xerxes esst bavard. Philippe parle _Xerxes.

- Filomena est souriante. Jona est désagréable. Filomena sourit _Jona.

- Peter est un bon chanteur. Gary ne chante pas bien. Peter chante _Gary.

Chapter 16: Verbs

French verbs are conjugated for Je, Vous or Tu, Il and Elle, and their plural forms. The French verbs are all based on four moods (namely: indicative, imperative, subjunctive, and conditional) and four simple tenses of compound perfect and progressive tenses (present, preterite, imperfect, and future).

In the French language, there are five main types of verbs, and these are: -er, -ir, -re/ -ir/ -oir, stem-changing, and irregular. Aim to understand the first three types of verbs so that you will find it easier to conjugate regular verbs.

Here are some examples: -er: aimer (to love), -ir: finir (to finish), -ir/ -re/ -oir: partir (to leave), rendre (to render), vouloir (to want).

Tenses

In the French language, there are four simple tenses, namely: Present, Past, Imperfect, and Future. Compound sentences are formed with the auxiliary "avoir" (to have) and past passive participle.

For example: J'ai regardé le drame. (I saw the drama).

Transitive verbs such as venir (to come), partir (to part), aller (to go), and mourir (to die) as well as all reflexive verbs are conjugated with "être" (to be).

For example: Je suis sorti de la maison. (I went out of the house).

You should also use verbal constructions to express immediate intention and recent accomplishment, such as aller followed by an infinitive and venir de (to come) followed by an infinitive, respectively.

For example: Je vais demain soir. (I will go out tomorrow night).

Moods

There are 5 verbal moods in French, namely: indicative, subjunctive, imperative, infinitive, and conditional. To form the passive voice analytically, "être" is used together with the past passive participle.

For example: Parlez-vous Français? (Do you speak French).

Compound Tenses

To construct compound tenses in French, use "être" or "avoir". Reflexive and reciprocal verbs are conjugated with "être".

For example: Samantha a levé sa main. (Samantha raised her hand).

A number of verbs are conjugated with "être" as well. This includes: aller (to go), devenir (to become), descendre (to descend), redescendre (to go down again), monter (to climb), remonter (to remount), rester (to remain), naître (to be born), mourir (to die), partir (to depart), retourner (to return), passer (to pass), sortir (to get out), revenir (to come back), venir (to come), and tomber (to fall).

Certain verbs that are usually conjugated with "être" can also be used with a direct object. In this case, the verb has to be conjugated with "avoir". Take note that the past participle should agree with the preceding direct object. However, if the verb is conjugated with "être", the past participle should agree with the subject.

For example:

Elle est descendue de l'avion. (She stepped down from the plane)

But...

Il a descendu deux valises. (He took down two suitcases).

Exercise

Try translating the following into French. Use a dictionary, if necessary:

- I am loved.

- I stood up.

- I sat down.

- I am taking a walk.

- I cut my fingernails.

- She came home late.

- She ate dinner.

- She is cleaning her room.

- She washed her hair.

- She will write a letter.

- He went up the roof.

- He is going down the stairs.

- He will die tomorrow.

- He was born 30 years ago.

- He climbed the mountain.

Chapter 17: Present Tense

In the English language, the simple present tense action refers to an action that occurs over an extended period of time, or an action that takes place at only one particular moment. For example: "I drive the car to work every day", and "She eats first, then you eat next."

Furthermore, in the English language, a compound construction called the present continuous or present progressive is used to show that the action is still happening, such as "I am driving the car to work right now". However, in French there is no such case. Instead, the verb that is conjugated in the present indicative can mean both ways, depending on the sentence context.

For example: Je danse bien (I dance well OR I am dancing well)

In French, the present tense is also sometimes used in place of another tense that i normally used in English. For instance, with the preposition "depuis" (meaning "for" or "since", an English people would say "We have been going to the university for three years." The compound verb "have been" in this sentence shows that the action is still ongoing. In French, on the other hand, you use the present indicative form of the verb: Nous allons à l'université depuis trois ans."

Formation

French verbs are divided into three conjugations based on their infinitive endings: -er, -ir, -re, an so on.

-er ending verbs

The verb that ends in -er is the infinitive (to... [something]), such as to eat, to sing, and to walk. The verb that does not have the -er is referred to as the "radical" or "stem".

To conjugate the -er verbs, you must take out the infinitive ending and replace it with the appropriate ending.

1st person: je -e (singular), nous -ons (plural)

2nd person: tu -es (singular), vous -ez (plural)

3rd person: il -e (singular), ils -ent (plural)

For example, to conjugate parler, you need to take out the -er and replace it with any one of the appropriate endings stated above, such as by saying "nous parlons" (1st person, plural).

All the regular -er verbs are conjugated based on this formula, with the exception of one small irregularity in verbs that end in -cer and -ger.

There is a pronunciation problem whenever the 1st person plural (nous) is conjugated to form the -ons if it is preceded by a g or c sound. It is this for this reason that the "e" is added after g or c (the latter of which is transformed into ç) to maintain the soft pronunciation of the g or c. These are referred to as the stem-changing verbs.

For example: the verb manger (to eat)

Je mange (I am eating), Nous mangeons (We are eating)

-ir ending verbs

Verbs that end in -ir are referred to as the "second conjugation verbs". To conjugate them, you omit the -ir and replace it with the present tense suffix: -is, -it, -issons, -issez, -issent. Keep in mind that in pronouncing the sounds, one s sounds like /z/ while two ss sound like /s/.

For example, to conjugate "finir" (to finish), you remove the -ir and replace it with the proper suffix, such as Je finis (I finish), Tu finis (you finish), vous finissez (you finish), il/ elle finit (he/ she finishes), and nous finissons (we finish).

Take note that there are certain verbs that do not follow this formula, such as ouvrir, sortit, partir, and dormir.

-re ending verbs

The irregular verbs are those which do not fall in the -er and -ir ending categories, such as -re, -oir, -ire, and so on. Again, there are some exceptions, such as prendre (to take), apprendre (to learn), surprendre (to surprise, and comprendre (to understand), which are conjugated the same way as the regular -re verbs in the singular, but not the plural.

For example: prendre becomes: je prends, tu prends, il/ ell prend, BUT nous prenons, vous prenez, ils/ elles prennent.

Exercise

Conjugate the following verbs:

- Je _chansons classiques. (aimer)
- Vous _le repas chaque jour? (preparer)
- Elle _sa mere à Belgium. (voir)
- Il _son travail. (finir)
- Nous _un magazine au salon (lire)
- Tu _ton argent sûr la table. (mettre)

Chapter 18: Future Tense

In the English language, you can form a basic sentence in the future tense by adding "will" before the verb. Forming the future tense in the French language is just as easy.

The Simple Future

In creating French simple future sentences, all you have to do is to add the following endings to the infinitive form of the verb: -ai, -as, -a, -ons, -ez, and -ont.

Here are some examples with the verbs that end in -er and -ir:

Parler (to talk): je parlerai (I will talk) tu parleras (you will talk), il/ ell parlera (he/ she will talk), nous parlerons (we will talk), vous parlerez (you (all) will talk), ils/ elles parleront (they will talk).

Choisir (to choose): je choisirai (I will choose), tu choisiras (you will will choose), il/ elle choisira (he/ she will choose), nous choisirons (we will choose), vous choisirez (you (all) will choose), and ils/ elles choisiront (they will choose).

For verbs that end in -re, omit the -e and retain the -r to form the past tense. Other verbs are irregular and they are the exception to this rule. Every time you encounter them, you will need to memorize them.

Here is a list of some of the irregular verbs with their stems in the future simple which you can start familiarizing yourself with: Avoir "to have" (aur-), Aller "to go" (ir-), Envoyer "to send" (enverr-), Falloir "need, must") (faudr-), Pouvoir "to be able to, can" (pourr-), Savoir "to know" (saur-), Venir "to come" (viendr-),

Vouloir "to want" (voudr-), Être "to be" (ser-), Devoir "should, must" (devr-), Faire (fer-), Pleuvoir "to rain down" (pleauvr-), Recevoir "to receive" (recevr-), Venir "to come" (viendr-), and Vouloir "to want" (voudr-).

The Recent Future

"to go" is the English verb that is used to express something that is going to happen in the immediate future. For example: "I'm going to the market to buy some eggs." In French, it is the verb "aller" that is used. Here is the French equivalent to the English statement above: Je vais au marché pour acheter des oeufs.

The verb "aller" can be used with other infinitive verbs that refer to anything that will take place in the immediate future. Here are some more sentence examples: Je vais manger ce ananas. (I am going to eat this pineapple), Elle va acheter un nouveau chapeau. (She is going to buy a new hat).

Exercise

Transform the following sentences into the simple future:

- Il chante au concert.

- Elle mange des croissants dans la cuisine.

- Vous aimez porter foulards Hermès.

- Ils portent des costumes noirs à l'église.

- Je fais cuire trois gâteaux.

Conjugate the following verbs into recent future:

- C'est Austin, qui _mon repas. (amener)

- Ma femme _un bon poulet frit. (preparer)

- Elle_ de_. (venir, partir)

- Je_ de_ mon travail. (venir, commencer)

- Son adversaire _furieux. (partir)

112

Chapter 19: Past Tense

The simple past is when you talk about a specific event that happened in the past. It is present in both English and French.

The Simple Past

This is the more commonly used past tense in the French language and it use used when you need to talk about an action that happened in the past and is now finished.

To form the simple past, you use an auxiliary verb, namely: avoir and être. The past participle of the verb avoir is "eu" (had), and of être is été (been). Generally speaking, the verbs that conjugate with the auxiliary être are the reflexive verbs and the intransitive verbs.

To make your sentence, you start by conjugating the auxiliary verb in the present tense,followed by the verb in past participle.

For example: aller (to go), past participle: allé

Je suis allé (I went), tu es allé (you went), il est allé (he went), elle est allée (she went), nous sommes allés (we went), vous êtes allés (you (plural) went), ils / elles sont allés/ allées (They went).

For French verbs ending in -er, the past participle is taken from the infinitive tense through replacing the ending with -é.

For verbs ending in -ir, the past participle is taken from the infinitive tense through replacing the ending with -i.

To conjugate with the auxiliary verb avoir, the past participle is not changed regardless of the subject; on the other hand, when the auxiliary verb être is necessary, the past participle is changed based on the gender as well as the number of the subject.

For example: L'avion est arrivé à 9 heures. (The airplane arrived at 9 o'clock)

In general, irregular verbs are usually transformed into the past participle by changing the infinitive ending into -u. For example: vendre (to sell) becomes vendu (sold), and vivre (to live) becomes vécu (lived).

Do not forget that there are also irregular verbs in the French past participle that do not fit into such patterns, such as "courir" (to run) which becomes "couru" (ran), and couvrir (to cover) which becomes "couvert" (covered).

The Recent Past

When you talk about the recent past, you are referring to an action that has just happened or has just finished. The French verb "venir" (in the present form) followed by "de", then the infinitive form of the verb.

For example: Il vient de partir. (He had just left), Ils viennent de quitter. (They had just left).

Exercise

Transform the following sentences into the simple past:

- Il chante au concert.

- Elle mange des croissants dans la cuisine.

- Vous aimez porter foulards Hermès.

- Ils portent des costumes noirs à l'église.

- Je fais cuire trois gâteaux.

Conjugate the following verbs into recent past:

- C'est Austin, qui _mon repas. (amener)

- Ma femme _un bon poulet frit. (preparer)

- Elle_ de_. (venir, partir)

- Je_ de_ mon travail. (venir, commencer)

- Son adversaire _furieux. (partir)

Chapter 20: Imperatives

The imperative form is used to state commands, express wishes, or give orders. In the French language, the imperative forms do not make use of tenses because they are straight to the point.

There are three imperative forms, namely: vous, tu, and nous. To create the imperative, you take the corresponding forms of the present indicative, omitting the subject pronouns.

Vous (2nd person plural)

"Vous" is used whenever you give an order to a group of people or to a person that you are not close with. The suffix -ez is attached afterwards.

> For example: Ouvrez! (Open!), Fermez! (Close!)

Tu (2nd person singular)

"Tu" is used whenever you nee to give an order to a single person, to a person you are close with, or to a child. The 2nd form singular of the imperative is used.

> For example: Ouvre! (Open!), Ferme-là! (Close that!)

Nous (1st person plural)

This is used whenever you need to say "let's (do/ go)!" By using this, you are including yourself in the group. The imperative form should have -ons attached to the end.

> For example: Faisons-le! (Let's do it!), Partons! (Let's go!)

Irregular Imperative Verb Forms

Être (to be): soyez, sois, soyons

Faire (to do): faites, fais, faisons

Avoir (to have): ayez, aie, ayons

Aller (to go): allez, va, allons

Negative Imperative

If you use the imperative with negative expressions, simply follow the usual negative construction (Chapter 13). Place the "ne" before the verb and the "pas" or the other negative modifier after it.

For example: Ne magnez pas cette pomme! (Don't eat that apple!)

Exercise

Fill in the blanks:

- Stacie, ___! (regarder)

- Sarah et Odette ___là. (rester)

- Rachel ___la porte! (ouvrir)

- _-nous là-bas! (regarder)

Chapter 21: French Travel and Business Words

In this chapter, you will learn some of the most commonly used French words when traveling and on business.

Travel Terms

The Airport and Plane:

➤ "Quelle est la raison de votre voyage?": What is the reason for your trip?

➤ "Combien de temps restez-vous à/ en/ au/ aux...?: How much time are you staying in...?

➤ Départs: departures

➤ Arrivées: arrivals

➤ Enregistrement des bagages: baggage check

➤ "Pouvez-vous ouvrir votre sac?": Can you open your bag?

➤ Décoller: to take off

➤ Atterrir: to land

➤ Faire une escale: to stop over

➤ Attachez votre ceinture: fasten your seatbelt

➤ Ne fumez pas or Interdiction de fumer: do not smoke or no smoking

- ➢ Restez assis: remain seated
- ➢ Éteignez tout apparell électronique: turn off all electronic devices

The Bus:

- ➢ Le bus: the bus
- ➢ Quartiers: neighborhoods
- ➢ Les lignes de bus: bus routes:
- ➢ Des excursions en bus: bus tours
- ➢ Un billet: a ticket
- ➢ Le conducteur de bus: the bus driver
- ➢ Distributeur automatique: automated ticket vending machine
- ➢ Le guichet: the ticket window

Entertainment:

- ➢ L'opéra: the opera
- ➢ Le concert: the concert
- ➢ Le ballet: the ballet
- ➢ Le cinéma: the movies
- ➢ Le théâtre: the theater
- ➢ La soirée: the party

Tourist Spots:

➤ La Joconde: The Mona Lisa

➤ Châteaux: castles

➤ Défense d'entrer: no admittance

➤ Photos au flash interdites: no flash photography

Theater:

➤ Les costumes: the costumes

➤ La pièce: the play

➤ La représentation or Le spectacle: the performance

➤ Monter un pièce: to put on a play

➤ Le rideau: the curtain

➤ La scène: the stage

➤ Le balcon: the balcony

➤ La tragédie: tragedy

➤ La comédie: comedy

➤ L'entracte: the intermission

Business Terms

The Professionals:

➢ Le président-directeur général: the CEO, managing director, or chairman

➢ Le directeur or la directrice: manager of a company or business

➢ Le gérant or la gérante: hotel, shop, or retaurant manager

➢ Le/ la propriétaire: the owner

➢ Le personnel: the employees or staff

Snail Mail and Phone Calls:

➢ Un mobile or un portable: a cellphone

➢ Une télécarte: a calling card

➢ "Allô": "Hello" on the telephone

➢ Dring dring: the French version of "ring ring"

Computers and the Worldwide Web:

➢ L'ordinateur: computer

➢ Le portable: laptop

➢ Le pseudo: username

➢ Le mot de passe: password

➢ Le navigateur: web browser

➢ Surfer le Web: to surf the Web

➢ Télécharger: to download

➢ Pièce de jointe: an attachment

➢ Envoyer: Send

➢ Insertion: Insert

➢ Fichier: file

Exercise

Construct French sentences based on the following scenarios.

● You need to look for the Louis Vuitton manager.

● You need to borrow a computer and surf the internet.

● Answer the telephone and tell them that you want to speak with the caller's company CEO.

● Tell your friend that you are going to watch a tragedy play first, then a comedy.

● Ask the bus driver about the price of the ticket and the route of the bus.

● Answer this question using French: "Quelle est la raison de votre voyage?"

● You want to know the directions to the museum that holds the Mona Lisa.

Conclusion

I'd like to thank you and congratulate you for transiting my lines from start to finish.

I hope this book was able to help you to understand and practice speaking French fast. The next step is to keep practicing and never give up.

I wish you the best of luck!

To your success,

Henry Ray

Printed in Great Britain
by Amazon